When the Sand Dries

A collection of poetry by

Alexandra Rose deMatteo

I dedicate this collection to you, the reader. My hope with sharing my observations is to open up a thoughtful dialogue with you and develop an environment based in love.

Contents:

Philosophical Approaches to Lifestyle   4-33

Scriptural Grounding   34-52

Outpour of Love   53-80

Philosophical Approaches to Lifestyle

"Mindful Midnights"

It's as if there is a film
A film over everything
Sealing each frequency
Within perfect harmony

The fade to zoom
Causes my eyes to marvel
The moments of clarity
Make all of life sparkle

Once I recognize the pattern
The image disappears
Always working towards understanding
On this revolving sphere

No matter how far
We can see with our eyes
The soul is the essential point
Each should centralize

Navigating the soul
Can be a scary journey
Walk with love
Be kind
Show yourself mercy

"July 4th, 2020"

Every day is Independence Day
I'm one independent woman
Taking advantage of my freedoms
May they forever be incumbent

I do the best with what I'm given
Extra creative and resourceful even
This country was founded on sacred rights, that I will fight for and believe
in

I am a woman of God and I defend my right
To be righteous and loving
To be my own knight

Do you acknowledge the rarity of democratic society, or act as if it is
experienced everywhere, since it breeds extreme anxiety?

Because we're obsessed with making the mighty dollar
Our system revolves around a life in neon color

Flash on flash
Vogue on vogue
The glamour of portrayed life makes originals go rogue

Praying one's authenticity is not stolen
While giving your vulnerability to the hands of the broken

Of course, it's easy to capitalize on the wounded
Does that mean you should focus on extorting the excluded?

I think not, that's a messed-up way to live
But most "democracies" act on nothing more than the derivative

Losing the meticulous values moment by moment
Until there are groups representing every single component

On this Independence Day, I feel especially grateful
To be surrounded by family, to be healthy, and to not be hateful

I know these circumstances don't translate universally, but the U.S.
Constitution said it intentionally: We the people of the United States, in
Order to form a more perfect Union, establish Justice, ensure...

"Hoodwinked for a Blink"

Insecurities speak for themselves
They love to be noticed
Subconsciously revealing the expression
of what you're like at your lowest

You become your own opponent
Fighting the urge of freedom
What is so horrible to accept?
When you have been bruised and beaten?

On the screen fitting into the scene
Editing reality to feel like a queen
Matriarch mentality comes from confidence
The dominance can't be without humbleness

The design of our confinement
Isn't the most elaborate labyrinth
It's your choice to conform
A testament to what you will restrict

What do you see when you look around?
How do you respond when things go south?
Do you let yourself meltdown?
To heal instead of drown?

"Acuity"

The way certain people view you holds more influence than others
Souls intentionally uncovered
Unable to be another

Even the subtle shades of my extravagant makeup exert enormous power
Drastically disrupting the status quo with new introspections every hour

Symmetrical smile, hair kept long
Passionately playing a game of expectation ping-pong

Whacking assumptions across the net, surprising each opponent

Helpless to their blind spot
Bugged eyes standing frozen

As the expression melts, all preconceptions follow
Courageous transparency can fill any space which is hollow

Listening for the echo
Waiting to feel the vibrations
Of someone rattling my mind, wanting to discuss life's foundation

Representing myself with clarity is a task to always be worked on
It's impossible to dictate impressions if you, yourself are withdrawn

"Unknowns of the Clone"

What do you do, when you can do nothing?
Do you instinctively close your eyes to imagine something?

The deep breathing reminds you, you're on your own
In the eye of the cyclone, you're forced to recall all you were shown

Harsh winds pull each limb in a different direction
Separating from center to make the decision of connection

As the velocity decreases, the body becomes whole
Translating ideas and plans to work toward your imminent goal

Will you fight and concede? Or are you determined to succeed?
It's healthy to see the color you bleed
How else would you know how to be what you need?

"Sweaty Therapy"

I feel like I'm running
Sprinting, on a treadmill
Conscious breath is my fuel
All movement around stands still

Each day blends together as it passes
Only colors are distinguishable
I wear my thoughts as makeup
To the thoughtful, those tones are visible

It's effortless effort
Moonwalking the same square
This weekend gave me a reminder of what I'm like on my own
Nothing can compare

Energetic and independent
Gaining perspective by the moment
Words powerfully guide behavior once they're passionately spoken

Running on the beach is much more my style
Facing adversity with ease
My existence is made worthwhile

Circulating salted air inspires the quality of my mind to improve
Exceeding my own expectations, while staying true to my groove

My groove needs an adjustment because the world has a new vibe
Tomorrow is never known but the path for each is inscribed

Laughing with my dad as we eat the dinner my mama prepared
Living under their roof is everything, despite my social life being spared

Covid-19 is a weird time
I'm doing my best to adjust
In order to keep my fire raging, running in any setting is a must

"Breathe in, Breathe out"

Ujjayi breathing
Such a miraculous technique
Meant to balance the body and cleanse the mind to think

Breath moving in through the nose
Filling up the lungs to their best
Sealing the lips softly
Listening to relieve all aspects of stress

Making an audible sound with the throat
Exhaling through the nose
Feeling the internal contraction
A rhythm begins to compose

Paying attention to the duration of your inhales and exhales
Attempting to equalize the counts as the diaphragm moves along it's trail

Whether you're sitting or standing
If you want to move or stay still
Your muscles are working, blood is circulating, cells are experiencing a
thrill

Taking advantage of the moment
It's your chance to commit
Figuring out your vibe
Why on Earth would you quit?

Expressing your determination every second you connect inwards
Noticing the bodily sensations
Being particular with your words

Meaning what you say
Doing what you mean
Practice on and off the mat
Washes away the unclean

Consistently exploring behaviors which make you feel your psyche
Surpassing your capabilities by pushing yourself to embody

Each time you embark on the excursion, you're practicing to be your
ultimate version

Innately igniting inclusion
Exploding traits of extraversion

Confident enough to share your breath with others who compete
Influencing those who need the help to conquer and defeat

The breath is yours to harness
You are already ahead by default
Share your kindness with the world
Breathe deep, wonderful thunderbolt

"The Question"

Conscious Existence = Conscious Breath
The equation has to be enough.
It's possible to be alive with death, when consumed by a negative outlook

All power is in the mind
Dictating metabolic processes
Fulfilling their intentional design
Replenishing targeted absences

Altering the chemistry to produce positivity
Where within your body do you hold the most sensitivity?

Sending your energy to those muscles
Mentally detailing your visuals
Physically feeling your breath move as you manage the detected signals

Sometimes the tightness
Takes time to release
Sometimes the tightness
Turns into instant peace

Thinking about how your emotional body settles into the physical as a
hobby
Effecting your energetic copy
Adjusting the connection when it's spotty

Learning the internal language to purify purposefully
Meditating and introspecting to better exist interpersonally

"Colors of the Water"

While analyzing reality
All I do is laugh
Surprisingly silent
Each moment like a photograph

Still and quiet
Every detail screams
Waiting to be seen
This is the extreme

Are we meant to feel this way?
To see so clearly?
To adjust our chemistry?
Even sincerely?

Sharing experiences and trusting in friends, brings out perspectives in
order to see through a new lens

Do you appreciate when you're questioned? Forced to deeply think?
That's when I connect the dots, my ideas start to sync

It always comes back to love, which is the root of all
Showering over us, a constant waterfall

Our duty is to give no matter the amount we receive
This is how we keep on track without the desire to deceive

We are the water
Blending together
From reflection to abyss
Depth is the only measure

When acting for humanity, you absorb a conclusive code
Exercising respect and patience requires a motivational mode

Practice makes perfect, that's what "they" say
Although, there is no perfection except in Yahweh.

We are here, existing
Living, to make a sacred choice
To love and cherish life
To balance the resonance of our voice

"Clarity Comes from Conversation"

Our countrymen and women continue to fight energetically for our
sanctified right to human equality

Protests, wars, demands on different levels
Vengeance violates as it pleases the devil

The oppressed or the oppressor
Is it possible to be both?
Within our borders we are equal
Immigrant and indigenous take the same moral oath

We can only work on what's ours
Improving quality with ample power
Connecting insights across time zones
Countrywide collaboration will make us prouder

Polarization can't be our foundation
Conversation is our invitation to realization

Do you want to revise the current goals of this visionary nation?
Will you be open-minded during this transformation?

"The Lady in Green"

I'm proud to be a native New Yorker, where self-determination sings loud
in our harbor
Ripples ruffle her robe causing her copper arm to reach higher

Flame is fulgent and golden
Shine is enshrined from the shore
Liberty leans towards us as we begin to restore

A new year is here
However, all issues of the present need resolution
Overcoming a sense of fear
Playing with your balance through this confusion

Immanuel Kant was nonchalant when syncopating the rhythm of our
international system

His many works explain every individual should behave by their own
moral commitments and wisdom

Viewing human nature as inherently good is at his base level
Then working our way up to the nationalistic power egos that wrestle

Do you think it's fathomable, to perceive morality as being dependent
upon the intentions and rules chosen to be applicable?

Historically, all attempts to shape a shared diplomatic network have been
based off of experimentation

Between the visions of
realism(structure), liberalism(process), and
constructivism/idealism(identity), there has to be a melodic combination

By deliberating and incorporating moral philosophy, logic, and ethics into
daily life, we EACH take responsibility for maintaining the sheath on the
communal knife

Our lady longs for our joint liberation
Inspiring us to discuss the terms of freedom for this hi-tech generation
Will you add your sound to the conversation?
Don't you want green to grow all over this federation?

"Many Layers to the Creator"

No human system is without flaw
We act in certain roles
Thinking we have the control
Naturally to submit our thumbs to scroll

Typing away, sharing passion
Hashtags bring about caution
Mostly trusting those who repost, instead of talking through the distortion

A Constitutional Republic, what a massive experiment indeed
Built upon rights given by God
Respecting humanity by respecting the principles adapted within our creed

Even the ones with piles of money also sweat for the system
Working tirelessly to uphold their fickle positions and abuse of capitalism

Obviously, there are worldwide disparities
I.e wealth, education, information, security, opportunity
But race being THE reason, is a true misjudgment of reality

We live in a world governed by energetic laws
Behaviors spiritually influenced by the unseen
By tapping inwards to our shared lifeline
You will outsmart this faulty machine

We all have access to breath
Which grounds us to reorientation
Following the clarifying sounds
Practicing to internally discuss reasons for causation

Bringing that knowledge forward
Proving to be made from the same
Wanting to be closer to each other by glorifying our creator with his many
names

"Earthly Realities"

Using your time wisely...
What does that even mean?
Showing up extra alert with a few cups of caffeine?

Trying not to miss any enjoyment, while being present in the moment?
In days of hardship, persisting through the omen?

What type of energy do you emit?
What do your thoughts reveal?
How can you adjust your behavior to concur with your personal ideals?

"Wiseman's Workplace"

Conversing with the wise does something extra to my mind
Specifically, when unexpected, a breadth of knowledge collects and aligns

Together, immersing fearlessly
The questions of life become clear
Bouncing information back and forth
Directing our theories to adhere

Even when there is a disconnect, I listen and stay present
Knowing you've had experiences in which you were able to circumvent

Everyone has the right to their worldview
Not everybody is right in their world view
But it's necessary to share perspectives, in order to perceive the answers
that will benefit the entire collective

Detaching myself from being anyone's judge
Allows me to show my respect
Viewing each story as sacred
Avoiding all neglect

"Train Ride Realizations"

The beat flows within
It feels completely normal
In car 7729, the NYC love portal

Looking out at the streets
An emptiness prevails
Sky pink and blue behind these intermittent rails

People are barbecuing
Others are sitting on their porches
Eyes on the smoke-filled air as they sharpen in focus

Car doors slam
Someone's yell is made fair
Despite all the glam
Some realities are too hard to bare

When you can only see the eyes
Every detail matters
Trying to read in depth
All potential intentions and patterns

A kindness must appear in order to gage my attention
I am not interested in feeling any sort of apprehension

Making the decision to feel comfortable on public transit, some would say
is a risk
I look up and notice four officers in the mix

Just doing their job
I feel safer when they're present
As a masked young woman, the obvious staring is frequent

"Challenges Arise from Many Angles"

Lines meet each other
Moving how they please
Problems find their solutions
In time and out of necessity

Nature runs its course
Unconcerned with personal struggle
Slowly or all at once
Morphing the model image of the puzzle

Trying not to double
Extra pieces keep appearing
Oy vey. Where do they fit?
One at a time to avoid tearing

Do you find complication overbearing?
How can you make stress fun?
Are you strong enough to ask for help before all is said and done?

"Chronicles of the Chambers' Chains"

Shame left alone leads to misplaced blame
A greatly understated truth

Impressionable beings
We seem to be
Never growing up from our vulnerable youth

Constantly trying to process the experiences and emotions
Reliving the pain of miscommunication
Causing the heart to decrease motion

With each unsettling moment
The chambers' locks fasten
Declining oxygen rich diffusion
Becoming one's own assassin

Working through the troubles as soon as they arise, can be the most
proactive way to keep your vessel from capsize

Even if something happened many years ago, facing the distress without
any residuals suppressed, unlocks the bound chains, giving oxygen access

Breathing with bravery
Responsibility is taken
Controlling what can be controlled
Perceptivity is awakened

"Parallels"

Mask on, mask off
The new universal game
You hear it from all angles
People claiming to meet the aim

Yes, intentions are everything
There aren't many solutions
Because we were given these conditions by global governance institutions

People seem to not feel the tight collar of power
Binding us to the leash of compliance
Narratives closing our throats
Igniting wildfire

Understanding the dark reality of what's really going on frightens most
Simply because it's "easier" to spend the time keeping ignorance close

Craving immediate gratification is different than being patient
Just like living a life of holy love is different from one of careless sin

Every day, I surrender my soul with the love of Hashem
By giving up control of "my own," I've concluded the wicked and evil
LOVE making themselves known

Masking and hiding
Until they are ready to shine
Constantly wreaking havoc
Keeping our realms intertwined

"Don't Bite"

Listening to "silence," isn't silent at all
Nature's calls are repetitive
Meeting a certain protocol

Dialogue among species is seriously popping off
All hiccups and coughs impart on the creative art

Everyone gets hungry around 6-7 at night
Trying to avoid another animal's eyes while they're thirsting for a bite

Teeth nice and sharp
Muscles strong and lean
Humans have the ability to pause and reconvene

In the untamed world, that's not how it rolls
Impulse dictates life, as each creature hunts and grows

Every family for themselves?
Why think like that as humans?
We're part of a global commonwealth
Effecting our environment by producing and consuming

The events going on in the world are no doubt discouraging and scary
Thankfully, the Judeo-Christian Word can be much more than just literary

Reading, speaking, reflecting upon the text is primary
Acting upon the content turns you interdisciplinary

Trying out new ways of living to possibly experience fulfillment
Setting up new standards definitely affected my temperament

A potentially deadly beast if the vision of democratic society were to
vanish
My primary duties are to love and apply scripture throughout all of this
madness

"Respect All Levels of the Chain"

This may be super weird, but I really love slugs
I think their markings are beautiful
In my heart, I'm part of their club

Leaving behind my slime
In a path that's real time
Distinguishing which way is mine
Out of the grime I will climb

The leopard slug shows her strut
The zebra slug slides by
Both glistening to get some bread
As they face the odds and defy

Living a life on the move
Searching for the best climate
Our textures aren't porous
We glide through life as the pilot

A hard animal to grasp
Unpleasant to prey upon
Attracted to food and comfort
We are the exact same pawn

Simultaneously used in this round
Different scale, same mission
Abiding by the rules of the earthbound
Bringing necessities to fruition

"Sneaky Snake"

I forget to remember, to be worried about the future
Already living through multiple computers
Logged in but unsure of the user

Online portrayal as real as can be
Unfiltered, straight forward
What you get is what you see

Not the most frequent poster
Commanding my degrees of composure
Of course, there are those cadets clambering and digging towards
disclosure

Wanting to be acknowledged
Wanting to have something to say
Of merit or not, utterances weave the community crochet

Rumpelstiltskin grins
At the one's turning gold into sin

Because they shed their shiny skin
For the benefit of their pixilated twin

"Always Room for One More"

Even when uprooted
Survival skills stay unpolluted
Adopting new knowledge bases
Communicating with the secluded

Symbolism speaks when gaging auras
I spend time singing with the birds to survey their techniques and morals

The goal is often the same
The route is always different
When living as one with the wild you realize everything is deliberate

Even the way each bird makes room for their fellow?
How do you let the stragglers in if their vibe ain't mellow?

They set their biases aside
They soften their pride
They choose not to divide
As each individual shifts from side to side

"Work Love, Love Work"

Today all I did was work
I suppose that's what it's all about
Whether it's out of the goodness of my heart or simply surviving for the
clout

No matter the circumstances
Humans are meant to work
Creating structure out of disorder by simplifying the complexities which
exist within the murk

We all have the ability to persevere through the challenge
Of educating ourselves to the point where we develop our own adage

But what good does the truth do if locked inside?
Fear. Doubt. Insecurity.
It's always time to override

The reward of the work depends on who you work for
Whether it's yourself, others, God, or the universe
A clear attention war

The recognition feels so good to receive
Especially when your effort is noticed
Generating a culture of minds that are bred to achieve and keep
themselves devoted

That is why we put in the work
To always feel prepared
Every moment is your shot
Love needs to be declared

"What are the Trains from Termination Station?"

Paying my dues
The repeated phrase of this feeling
I've just been laid off
This taste is most unappealing

Nothing to do with my aptitude
A disappointment no matter the reason
I left a spicy impression, but that's how it goes during Covid season

Many others are in my position so I can't feel too unique
Each organization restructuring their plans to accommodate the attack
An immaterial sneak

Some businesses are forced to close; Some businesses are forced to merge
Some businesses are booming, fueling the markets to upsurge

New to the world of the Nasdaq
Examining the bull and bear tug
Paying attention to the money flow
It's impossible to unplug

Trading never stops
Exchanges of all sorts
Leaping through continents
Deliberately coerced

Being told where is smart to invest, while there is so much unrest
Power seats getting filled with the greedy, lonely, and depressed

We are a country of thoughtful minds, having our livelihoods dictated by a
system whose opinion is outdated
Investing in kindness can make situations less complicated

Despite the immediate sadness
Getting let go was a pleasant experience
My boss called to check-in
Offering sincere reassurance

Some confidence has been restored
Already back to the drawing board
I don't know what stop is next
I'm ready for the unexplored

"Zestful Lens"

Woke up for another day
Metallic clouds fill the sky
Poured my cup of black coffee
Mindful as the hours pass by

Ample ambition overwhelms the air
Focused with clear tunnel vision
Embracing all emotions with prayer, to meet each second with precision

Starting from square one again
Prioritizing my happiness
Where will I be the most useful?
How will I get in my practice?

Given the gift of time, to personally mandate my schedule
Being brave enough to reach out and make the most of my potential

As a woman of multiple professions, I see opportunities to make
impressions
Influencing love in life
Acknowledging the sacrificed concessions

Assigning utilities to determine value
Creating the integral solution
Steering away from anything shallow
Avoiding the possibility of illusion

Conducting in-depth research is essential to making the best offer
I'm negotiating with the Father as if he isn't innately the author

Providing me with experiences
Some lasting others halted
Faith keeps us curious
Love keeps us vaulted

Jumping around the globe
Putting my lens into scope
Expressing combined cultures reassures the sentiment of hope

Knowing my path will be revealed
Right now, I'm meant to relax
To be patient with the Lord and examine the abstract

"What's My Age Again?"

My childhood room hasn't changed much over the years
Aside from the cardboard cutout of Jesus, one of my Jewish sisters got me
for cheers

Every time my eyes look over to the life-size "profile" of His sacrifice
It's Pesach, Lamb's blood is marked on all doors to suffice

Showing my faith by acting it out
Believing I will be taken care of
Dismissing everyone's external doubt to provide 100 percent of my love

I don't know how to describe this feeling
Age is truly just a number
The more time I spend in here
I swear I'm getting younger

Freshly brewed coffee fills the house
The most potent and cozy alarm
Roommates B. & D. are off to work as I stay home and tend to our farm

Tons of activities to keep me busy
Creating a career is a process
Centering to the Lord for guidance
With many unknowns, it's hard not to stress

Meditating in the finite world to have access to the infinite
Building strength with breath
Controlling to be a better person

Tapping into the ultimate source of energy and wisdom
Enjoying the intensity of the force
Developing a sense of altruism

Attention to the breath is attention to existence
Surrendering to the subtleties
Meeting resistance with acceptance

"Wash your Hands"

Preoccupying thought with diverse sources of news
Tasked with making sense of rhythm in the midst of blues

Desperate to hear the bass bang through all that is out of tune
Draining out the tolerant toxins to remain unanimously immune

What's the dominant virus here?
Will the vaccine be?
Will democracy disappear?
What's the price to keep speech free?

"When the Sand Dries"

I love when firm sand cracks beneath my feet
So hard on the surface but brittle underneath

Much like our international system, various footprints cover the landscape
One indent building upon another
Manufacturing a noticeable reshape

Only until the wind blows and the tide rolls over, do the man-made
masterpieces have their chance of exposure

The ground is now uneven
Causing stability to weaken
Driven by societal pressures
Living in the Garden of Eden

Humans have gone throughout history, with time remaining a mystery
No way to date the start and end
Simply breathing is a victory

In every country, no matter the status, the struggle for all is the same
Making a living to take care of the family, while trying to maintain a
positive frame

Here in the United States
We truly are no different
We are capable of finding understanding without getting too frustrated and
belligerent

We're playing a petty game of diversion
Clickbait is a direct inversion
Dismissing the lessons of the Lord is creating the most detrimental
aversion

Hearts to turn cold
Minds to be controlled
Bodies injected and mangled
If love is not acted upon and told

Scriptural Grounding

"Tropical Trumpets"

The tropical storm has brought a huge wave
Clouding the skies
Brightening some minds

Simply listening to the almighty producer
While he graciously performs on the spiritual sound mixer

The lyrics of the birds
Sampled to the beats of the breeze
Feeling the pulse internally
Relying on the winds gust through the trees

The light suddenly shines in
Then it seems to fade
Back and forth
Until the human being feels compelled to evade

Daytime is ending
Which means darkness for hours
Hashem is behind the booth
Synthesizing Shabbat's power

Until tomorrow at sundown, my mind is not my own
I'm meant to show gratitude and reflect upon the theological throne

I love and respect the Holy Trinity
Hashem, Yeshua, and Holy Spirit
May you and your angels continue to show us all affinity without any limit

The most magical musicians to ever exist
Permanently playing your natural instruments so your creations have the
chance to enlist

"Honest, Simple Shabbat"

Once you see it
You never unsee it
The vibe of the day

Twirling around, intentionally forming as an impressionable ball of clay

Surrounded by green
Gazing into the landscape
Watching the stillness entirely manifest

As if we are in the age of the ape, using the stars as our compass

Resetting to realness actively shapes the trees
Dramatically blooming and curating all types of leaves

Frame by frame
Elements remain the same
But in reality
There is endless movement

At that micro level
All edges bevel
We simply live for self-improvement

Making decisions about where we'll go and how we are going to
prosper...

Building relationships
Being authentic
A good vibe attracting monster

Have you tried reciprocating trust and generosity?
Love is able to foster

Looking at the mountain
Meet the horizon
My body aligns to perfect posture

Giving us the gift of awareness
Allowing us to appreciate your beauty
I thank you for this wonderful life and to be one of your creations, truly

"L'chaim- To Life"

Partying for the weekend in a stranger's home leaves much time for discovery

Each room is dressed in descriptive photos, revealing humanity is pretty lovely

Not recognizing a single feature displayed among the property
Admiring this wholesome families' expression of American-made quality

The house is a preacher
Stars and Stripes pattern the estate
Members of this family dedicate their lives to protecting our country's fate

Entertaining mostly Jewish people within this Christian environment
Produced profoundly beautiful exchanges, resulting in collaborative enlightenment

On this Shabbat
The density is heavy
God's love circulates among all of his creations immensely

"Faithful Fortress"

I felt the click
Immediate
Vibes made to flow
A continuous tick

Eyes so blue
They reflect as ice
Conveying experiences but lacking knowledge of Christ

Everyone has their own path and journey to how they make sense of
global history and society

Personally, my Israeli adventures brought me to value scripture
Reading, praying, discussing to curiously define the components of my
mixture

Until I was exposed to the Gospel of Jesus Christ
I didn't understand the magnitude of the ever-holy sacrifice

Empathizing to grasp
The personified perfection
Empathizing to grasp
Mankind's pattern of deflection

Our sins are proportioned
Our sins make us human
Our sins bring us together
Within his holy union

Without the Son's devotion to the almighty Father, we would not be able
to combat the evils set upon us to slaughter

Experiencing the boundless braid between the Old Testament and the New
Adding the teachings of the Talmud and the Kabbalah
Concocting the ultimate spiritual brew

Realizing each sentence is written by the same author
Guiding the reader to their knees extends the significance of the offer

All of this power given to us through the Lord
Exercising faith with loving intent is central to hearing what's unheard

It's like when the sun melts all of the ice away
Our souls become cleansed
Feeling empowered not to be led astray

That's why I make choices where I continuously commit
Showing my obedience out of respect, It's my conscious right to emit

Getting to know the Word is a task of a lifetime
Could studying with strangers become your natural paradigm?

A special energy is produced once the Gospel projects out of one's throat
Keeping the faithful safe on the castle side of the moat

"Ha'aretz"

I think about the ways I've changed on the daily
My routine and my mindset, I constantly compare to the Israeli

To be analytical, resilient, and of course loving
There is nowhere else on Earth as historic and becoming

Everywhere I go, I radiate the vibes
Within me are my ancestors
A lineage extending from the tribes

I am extremely grateful to be a Messianic Jew
Building a personal relationship with Hashem, Yeshua, and the Holy Spirit
too

Do you love experiencing life?
Every moment of every day?

When spending time in "The Land," you come to understand the
prestigious price which is paid

During my lovely twirls and when I seem to wander
I pray for ALL people to be safe and to prosper

The location of sensation
The soil of soul
Establishing common ground, so one day we may all be whole

Fault lines overlap, concentrating the current
I have vowed and will continue, to forever be observant

"True Flight"

My dad loves to say: "There is no better lie than the truth"
To make your shake with whey is to make your martini with vermouth

Necessities are necessities
Preference is preference
Experimenting with your identity without ever taking severance

No amount of perceived value can take the place of your worth
My surname means "Of Matthew"
I've been Messianic from birth

Without knowing the Trinity
Without acting accordingly
I was led to question reality and get my answers mercifully

Over time, the liveliness of scripture became very distinct
Depicting how Jesus intertwines humanities' zipper and connects us all to link

Subjection to sin is a part of our dimension
Only He can judge our responses and choose our paths of ascension

Every moment lived in the earthly body truly matters
Each thought brings about future events
Dictating life to climb up the moral ladder

Maintaining an eagle's eye as you soar among the clouds
Solving problems honestly
Leading the Lord to feel proud

We each have the same shot to make our creator notice
Aiming to appreciate, our minds and hearts will stay open

"Being Told Can Be Annoying"

Do you let others pressure you? Or do you say fuck off?
Totally depends on my mood, I'm Anastasia from Romanov

Rooting from my family tree to find my way back home
I take my bindle to the lands of the plentiful
Feeling free to roam the globe

Awaited with open arms
I am who I claim to be
Hearing all the piercing alarms expecting to assess my destiny

I can be my own worst enemy
Distraction can make me miss opportunity
Only Hashem knows what's best for me
That's why I live to give gratuity

In the form of smiles and dialogue
You can tell by my eyes, I'm genuine
As a daughter of the Alpha dog, I have a sense of compassion built-in

What a gift it is…to be able to personally relate others
Pure etiquette and kindness help to fully connect with any culture

Some people carry demons around because they have met them personally
Sewing their stripped innocence together as they pick out their fabric
urgently

Any quick stitch to look incognito so I may not see their wounds
Repeating the wrongdoings felt, inhaling inescapable fumes

You know what you know
For many, it's prolonged sadness
Anchoring to God's light projects that darkness will vanish

Loving the trial and error
Falling short is expected
Using each choice as a mirror
Changing the ingrained methods

Figuring out your style of learning to be your own best teacher
Making it exciting to apply the material
Becoming a true self-healer

"Energy Can Only Be Exchanged"

An energy has been lurking around me
Insanely influential and mischievous
Making me want to rebel at all moments
Turning my gaze insidious

Obviously unambiguous
I know exactly who you are
You've been sent to test my will and leave me with a noticeable scar

Attempting to convert my frequency to your dull end of the spectrum
I am automatically provided with the antidote which combats your vibey venom

Asking for assistance as I restrain from committing acts of shame
Asking for forgiveness, I'm human, sometimes I miss my aim

Luckily the target is infinite, as long as my relationship with the Lord remains intimate
Through realizations and self-corrections, God's love is eloquent

"Breaking the Law"

Romans 8 explains: the love of Hashem, which is in the Lord, is certain.

Meanwhile, throughout most of time and space, the earthly prince attempts to evoke each beast of burden

He feeds on cheating our tastes
He gets high on leading the innocent to replace, their wholesome vitamins with supplements that are deceitfully laced

False labeling and product placement
Strategically pervading your figure
How can you feel comfortable to speak your mind when everything is considered a trigger?

Following the muse of the spirit, will lead your voice to deliver
Invariably supporting your spunk whether or not the setting is familiar

Assurance stems from analysis
Deducing postulates like in calculus
Never arriving at zero
Always reasoning through randomness

Examining the instantaneous changes which are turning our systems blasphemous
Once your relationship with the Lord is made, existence is handled with graciousness

"Lost Soul Landscape"

Crossing the bridge
Looking out into nothing
Gave my body chills so I just kept trusting

You said, "We must be in Heaven" and it made me think
That we are experiencing what some have at their brink

Absolute grayness
No life in sight
A heavy mist
Yearning for light

I quickly replied "No way, Heaven is plentiful"
We laughed and agreed
I continued to be skeptical

I thought about the deeper meaning of why we were shown this panorama
Significant at this point in time because society is experiencing significant
trauma

Studying the spiritual Samba, so my footwork is in time with the karma
Moving through each historical saga to interpret this unfolding drama

The fact of emptiness was something I needed to see, in order to
comprehend that space existing on the hierarchy

I'm glad we got to share that scene and talk about it after
I appreciate your chill attitude mitigating the magnitude with laughter

"Checked by The Architect"

How can things be fine in one moment, then turn to such shit?
In the blink of an eye, it becomes too hard to tell the real from counterfeit

Material on the surface level
Even angels can get jealous
Ultimately gratifying the devil

The leader of the fallen wants us to live in his world
As we wrestle and tremble our souls are comedic to whirl

For entertainment?
As a trophy?
To make a mockery of?
And turn us unholy?

That's his plan
To use and dispose
Do you know the perspicacious practices of your shadow?

Darkness follows when light shines
Maintaining the contrast
Between evil and kind

We've been given His divine guides
So that we may distinguish each possible sign
Reminding us that we are not to be left as vines
Growing directionless within our confines

"Placed in the Pace of Progress"

Slowing down
To accommodate the times

Reduced interaction
To read between the lines

Once the epiphany resonates in the mind, do you display an interest in
protecting mankind?

If the answer is no, just know we will prevail
If the answer is yes, we forgive their betrayal

We're living in the storm of Jonah and the Whale
Which Hashem bestowed to directly impale

All trapped together in the belly of our savior
Preserved and enlightened so we may be meek in nature

Once we get tossed up
We'll be free to breathe and speak
Faithfully living like Jonah
With trust we shall proceed

"Nighttime Tales"

Night watcher
Night watcher
How do you watch me?
Do you protect my sanity?
Secure my humanity?

I've been waking up in sweats
With horror in excess
Only asleep do I see such sadness

I woke up to pray
Speaking to you to protect me
Needing to differentiate heinous fantasy from harmonious reality

The dream sphere is meaningful and declares a powerful tale
To what degree is that imagery painted to scale?

I don't know exactly what you are trying to tell me
I guess the coded messages correlate to our never-changing state of
fragility

Many are playing around, trying to be their own "God"
Only until they realize they're already a forever fraud

Manipulating energy to make selfish desires happen
Trying to make the most of their clock with whatever trends are in fashion

The vulnerability of life is an inescapable truth
I'm distressed without your lullaby
My mind needs to be soothed

Saturating me with love even when perceived otherwise
Lord, you are my night watcher
I rely on you to advise

"Choosing God is Choosing Yourself"

Listening to Kanye speak on our collective dismissal of humanity
Sharing our obligation to the Trinity, as we shed light on some global insanity

The life of the unborn, such a controversial issue
Souls are souls, at some point the earthly course ceases to continue

To have command over one's choices is an essential human right
Paying the price for your own sins is a genderless and inevitable fight

But how can the individual take responsibility for the species?
-By forming a relationship with themself and not yielding to mesmerizing freebies

Knowing nothing is without cost, consequences connect our web
Responsibility to oneself and to every living being are one in the same step

I'll never be done investigating the character and ways of my master
Tactically training to detect sinful seduction like a forecaster

Never pumped with birth control
I committed early to the natural route
I still had times where I took "Plan-B"
Scared not all swimmers pulled out

To be a mother now, I'm not ready
I'm 24, single, and perfectly happy
Plus, abstaining from sex makes all the men crazy

Choosing commitment
Rather than fake fulfillment
I pray I am strong enough to resist

Serving the flesh
Opposed to serving the sacred
Is a reason we debate existence

You can only choose one
Please approach with care
Will you serve; Self (man) or God?
Where does your heart pair?

49

"Time Seems to Move Slower When Fasting"

Bare to feel my nature, rumbles trembling within
The emptiness inside translates to wholeness under the fortified skin

Not drinking a single drop
Saliva is in natural production
Steering away from all attachments which would normally end in
seduction

Chewing only words, swallowing only thoughts
Resetting my body and mind to be one with my open heart

Repenting for my sins isn't just a one day of year event
I continuously fall short
Adjusting my behavior to supplement

The difference with Yom Kippour
Is the preceding 10-day period of "Awe"
Rosh Hashanah marks the new year
Introspecting and atoning to feel raw

In order to make amends for my wrongdoings of the year
I hop in the memory machine and shift that baby into gear

Reliving every missed step
Asking Hashem for forgiveness
Before He evaluates and decides my fate, I will show him the strength of
my commitment

All people are equal in the eyes of our Lord
We're all free to choose what we may, but expected to untangle our own
cord

Celebrating our new covenant
Undergoing rebirth and renewal
The Torah is here to universally inspire
Filtering the spectrum for approval

Ending tonight, my 10 days are up
Uncomfortable now, but full of God's love
Soon I will be fed, time will be as usual
Paying extra attention to the light and the beautiful

"Cast a Line"

Hungry for the catch
Waiting for something to attach
Watching the surface scratch
While I reel in what was latched

Picking up the empty net
My eyes start to tear
Just as I wipe my cheek, the Son of God appears

Walking by the Sea of Galilee after withstanding maximum temptation
Willed with the love of Hashem to be the path of our salvation

He says to us: "Follow me, and I will make you fishers of men"
We immediately left our nets and followed the Lord, Amen

Hearing the gospel from His lips
Scripting in detail all of His tips
Multitudes of people are faithfully transfixed
I am a fisher of men, nourishing entire ships

Matthew 4

"Listening Requires All Senses"

Hashem does not have to speak to you directly for you to hear him

Rotating the dial
Assuming were tuned in
Sharpening our eardrums to recognize His sound on a whim

We're on a scavenger hunt
Clues left by the Lord
Sending disguised messages so the conversation is on and off the record

What happens if we have trouble decoding?
Will we be ignored?
Will you try a different delivery so the message can be properly applied
and stored?

I know I have to be patient but sometimes your reply is delayed
I wrongfully look for statements
In the subtleties, your responses remain

You loved me first
It's my honor to love you back
Giving us your words so we may sing along to your soundtrack

To listen to Hashem's voice
I observe Scripture
To listen to Hashem rejoice
I immerse myself in His entire picture

A Kingdom of conscience
The ideal world to be
Each soul deliberately acting with love, righteousness, respect, and
integrity

Outpour of Love

"Grapple"

The abstract
Of my mind
Gets tangled
And blended

Morphing in shape
Ever-changing
Never mended

Staring into space
So bright and mysterious
The variation of darkness
Makes nothing out of distance

I think about your smile
My cheeks start to blush
As if you've just shifted me into
gear and popped the clutch

Acceleration with no clear destination
Entertaining this jolting flirtation
Admiring your affirmations
Hoping to stir up comprehensive conversation

I think you really like
Having access to my mind
Picking up the valuable information with the ability to strike

You pin me down
To where I'm submissive
I like to share
Completely permissive

"Old School"

You ask how you know me
As if you don't remember
We used to flirt back and forth
Like we were on some kind of bender

Substance was a rarity
I didn't seem to care
All I wanted was your attention and to take off my underwear

Since then, I have evolved into a woman who values meaning
Constantly analyzing my actions while adjusting and feeling

I choose depth over lust with someone that I kiss
Patience and discipline definitely intensify the bliss

I know you may not want to wait or see the value in my choices
But I want to get to know you and all of your various voices

I hope you can agree with me
Our chemistry is fire
It's honestly just time and respect that I require

"Revealing the Real"

My thoughts unravel on the tip of your tongue
Buds break down the essence to swallow my intricacies with love

Your smile speaks to me while the taste settles in
Reactions and responses are those of an electric violin

Soulful and candid
Entirely enthralling
Chills run around my spine
Particularly stalling

In no rush to move
Magnifying my mood
The notes you play are heard with natural certitude

You put my words to melody
While holding my hand steadily
Both experiencing therapy by detangling each other sensibly

"Line in the Dirt"

This feeling is fleeting
Your back is turned to me
Rapidly drifting away from each other
I guess this means I'm free?

Not tied to you
My ribbons are curled
Locks slide out from in between your fingers to restore all emotions that
were whirled

Your best friend?
I don't think so
Maybe your best means to an end whose love was too easy for you to
extend

I knew you were cheated so I wanted you to feel worthy
Maybe that was too nice, it put me on an unfortunate journey

From sharing our affection, to feeling ignored by your deflection
I respect your place in life but want no more of this intervention

You made me feel like we were beginning to entwine
Now I'm completely inclined to romantically unbind
No longer putting your needs before mine
We desire different things, you so clearly defined

"Views"

He tells me
You need to adjust your mindset
Because I said
I want my kind of love duet

He tells me
You really are the rarest dove
It's not about what you want
It's ordained from above

It's about what you deserve
You have earned the world
For someone who emulates your worth
Keeping you one with the Earth

Many won't get you
Most won't try
They want you to fit their mold
While they pretend and lie

I said in response
You're so right
It's hard for me to act on my worth
When I'm held perfectly tight

I get caught up with providing love, even to the undeserving
Where I move on so quickly, feeling each intense sting

I keep cutting them off
Because they all disappoint
Maybe that's cold
It's my strongest vantage point

"Smoking Gun"

Sometimes
I close my eyes
Just to see your face

To remember that look
In your eyes
I hopelessly retrace

Going over each line
Longing to make them bold
Emphasizing romance
As I put on a blindfold

Submitting to the heart is a difficult skill to master
I'll do anything to avoid an emotional disaster

You looked at me
As if I were a crystal
So clear and so polished

Full of energy
Full of love
Waiting to be harnessed

That's where you went wrong and completely missed the signal
You failed to see my edges
I'm one deadly pistol

"Snowball Effect"

There is something about you I get reminded of constantly
You didn't see me as I wanted
I held on, honestly

Letting my calluses bleed
Recalling every detail
Of the way you looked when I lifted my veil

Completely vulnerable
Our expressions were matching
I should've known then you'd have trouble attaching

Now that I've said, "enough"
I miss your voice extra
Your energy transported me straight to another era

One where it was my turn to be timeless
Instead of succumbing to the demands of an orchestrated virus

I wanted to spend time with you
It all got screwed up
The swell was too much to handle
I got caught in the buildup

"Book Ends"

Do you feel that division?
Regret is in remission
No longer questioning my precision
I've reasoned with my decision

There's a chance you were honest
But it's very unlikely
Even if you made the impression
I was choosing wisely

I wasn't at all surprised reality made you flee
Especially because I shared my most tender thoughts and abstinence plea

I never fully explained why I make these sacred choices
This experience is a prime example of how I utilize my voices

You probably thought my honesty
Was weird and frequent
I want to date a friend
Not a scared delinquent

I weed out the incompatible
Each moment I'm authentically myself
One day there will be my matching end on the bookshelf

"Novel Navigation"

Some connections are meant to be made
Strangers one second, quickly changing direction

As my hair blows at your door
Waves build up the rapport
Moment by moment, a feeling grows impossible to ignore

Inquiring about your background
Past adventures proving to be profound
You seem to have it all figured out
Bringing rain to end the drought

Even though we have very different practices and realities
Our exchanged insight levels us with Socrates

Philosopher, theologian, dreamer
Relishing in existence as symbiotic teachers

Meeting challenge with ambition
Harmonizing human cognition
Being open with each other as we work through new definitions

One glance and I was attracted
Your fresh fade set the tone
Instant exposure to your culture
Grateful for your unknown

"Atmospheric Anomaly"

After each rapid-fire question my mind needed to collect
In order to provide you with the best answer to obtain your upmost respect

A beach night with you was as electric as the lightning
Bolts brewing inside the clouds
Crashing down, meeting the ground

To be felt
To be seen
Each ray of white light flashed a versatile vaccine

Treating many ailments
Filling many voids
Enhanced exhilaration
Once simultaneously struck by the compatibility steroid

Intense but not overwhelming
Suspenseful without worry
Easing into each other without any bit of hurry

Effortless exchanges
Your kindness radiates
I'm captivated by your attributes
Many of your traits, I seek to emulate

"The Standard Setter"

Hanging up the phone
Confidence on boost
Spending time with you is the best
Pure trust is induced

I let you in completely so that I turn inside out
The tenderness of my humanity roots with you, blooming sprouts

Bulbs in the shape of thought
Stems in the shape of reason
Being friends to each other first keeps our hearts in cohesion

You speak to me with honesty
Sometimes it makes me nervous
No matter what goes on in our worlds, we will always be at each other's
service

You are someone that I love
That I care for and adore
Perpetually proving to be righteous and honorable to your core

Opening up about others and my exceptions of a lover
Feeling your earnest encouragement to have trust for another

Why should I trust when their kindness isn't there?
They look at me and stare
Only my body they crave to share

You paddle out to the depths my mind so we can surf the same wave
Barreling through affection and love
All of our memories are safely saved

"The Luck of the Draw"

A wild night out
Swiping left, occasionally right
Hopping from app to app
Praying to not see the same pics twice

You can't feel their energy
It's a poor game of jeopardy
Do I trust AI to deliver a board of synergy?

Maybe once or twice, I engaged with someone who enticed
Cautious of my time spent playing
Won't negotiate my asking price

Trying not to miss the real vibes
I take my head out of the virtual
Keeping an eye out for my jackpot
Turning luck entrepreneurial

"Hopeful Heart"

I'm not scared
If anything, I'm ready

Too ready to let go
Too ready to lock in
Holding out to avoid being attacked by sly sin

I want what everyone wants
To love and to be loved
Simple, honest, yet so much deceit is involved

Playing by my own rules
Makes the games more fun
Keeping each man on their toes as they think they've already won

Won what?
Makes no sense to me
Legs remain closed
Heart remains open
Engineering ebbs and flows
I am the ocean

Transparent and reflective
The abyss of love and life
Paving my own way so one day
I can be the most wonderful wife

I'm excited to create a shared adventure, with unconditional love at the
center
A true friendship, the most courageous venture

Maybe my craving to be in love is lustful?
Maybe it's pure?

Either way, I know I'll have the experience once I mature further

We all deserve to be seen
We all deserve to be known
Maintaining self-love and discipline holds up a hopeful heart unavailable
for loan

"What Lies Across"

Millions of dots
Enter the water
Creating their own waves
Becoming one with another

Viewing the recoil
Which causes a smack
A noise so loud, repeating on playback

Each morsel that drops is completely unique
It is up to the eye to make use of the bleak

Watching the individual
As it joins the collective
Seamlessly combining elements
Displaying the true perspective

Mayim, Water, H2O
Embedded in each living thing
Our system connects to grow

Within and excreted
Only LOVE is as universal
Our dependence on BOTH is the point of transversal

"Soul Mining"

Does morality usually win?
What's the strategy to outsmart the kingpin?
Do you feel comfortable in your own skin?
Can you be healthy without being thin?

Chiseled jaw
Thick waist
Twerking around town
My aura takes up space

Owning my presence
Embracing past disgrace
In control of my essence
Adding love to the human race

Letting go of lust
Training to be robust
Awaiting to be dug into like the Earth's crust and watch my surface spray
into dust

"Every Pot has a Top"

As a young girl
I had wished for this time
To not be on anyone's schedule
To put myself on the grind

I sometimes get stuck
Keeping up the motivation
"Thank you for your application, we're going
with someone else from across the nation"

Apply, Apply...
Deny, Deny...
Ego is bruised but not shook or terrified

Someone will choose me
I know that to be true
Thirsty to be back to work
Hungry like at a barbecue

Bills buy me wings
Coins buy me sauce
How can I test my potential, if I am left and tossed?

A side salad type of girl
Complimenting my main meal
Feeding myself soundbites of love
Bonding with the real

As a young woman
I value this experience
To hold myself accountable while assessing my obedience

"A Mission of Aviation"

The earthly view of Apollo's guide
Allows us to carefully watch him
Move the sun across our submerging sky

Pushing the days into nights
Illuminating enclosed activity
So that we may savor the details and profoundly practice tranquility

Beauty exists in every morsel of the planet
Do you try to make observation and comprehension some of your many
talents?

Like Apollo, pulling back the bow
Arrow promptly spears into the bullseye
Feeling the flow, in sync with the tempo
Transitioning innocently into a butterfly

As aerodynamics self-programs
My flight distance is limited
Striving to use my might and assist Apollo with his disciplines

"Messages have Many Meanings"

Receiving your message of kindness
Made me eager to reply
"I hope you have a fabulous day
Thank you for being you! LY"

Especially since it's 10/10
You encouraged me to feel one hundred
Completing my essence, perceiving omnipresence
As if a volcano had just erupted

Magma is spewing into lava
Autumn colors add the drama
Setting the stage for a very powerful opera

Hashem is the lead
Glorification does the deed
Giving us all what we need
To perform with love and succeed

"Encore"

Where are you now?
My tears are wondering
The standing ovation for your final bow
won't stop this curtain from closing

With your spotlight off, the show still goes on
Currents pulse among neurons
Stimulating, to signal that you're not gone

You're everywhere but nowhere
I stay energetically aware
Putting your name in my prayer
Feeling your love as a flare

"Decisions and Destinations"

Do you think "empty space" is actually unoccupied?
When you die, does your soul divide or become unified?
Do your earthly choices determine where you qualify?
When you die, will you deny or glorify?

Our ever-expanding universe
Our ever-expanding life force
Exploring the empty with everyone's energy
Connecting us all to our loving source

"BFF"

How many times a day do you speak to your favorite person?
Are you able to put both talking and listening into proportion?

An exchange of emotion
Too comfortable to approach with caution
With everything in common
Both laughs lead to exhaustion

Happiness prevails
Naturally among us
Discussing life with trust
Our love ceaselessly combusts

"Blood is Thicker than Water"

Hashem is at hand for all things
Even when he uses people to yank others' heart strings

Some conversations can have the most honest intentions
But the delivery is too hectic and turns the content toxic

Digesting that poison so it rests as an elixir
Love, tears, reflection, and action
Bringing the wound to blister

Bursting out emotion
Forming a natural barrier to infection
Letting go of expectation to heal in the most perfect fashion

Your family loves you
That is a fact of your life
Each member has their own way of
conveying the bond which exists
through the afterlife

My way is to show you
I will always be your sister
I'm here to respect and love you
To listen to your perspective and be your uplifter

"Inverse"

I love that you love me
You love that I love you

"25 Years to Life"

Thinking about your love brings tears into my eyes
I wish I could have seen your face when he proposed from the skies

Covering you with love
Every second of everyday
You know you can't get rid of him
B. A. N. D. S. is here to stay

You understand each other
You set the perfect example
On how to create a family unit in which love and joy are ample

I have acquired endless things from you
But it's the wholehearted love, I cherish most
The energy you two produce permeates at a tremendous dose

Anyone can feel it
I'm so blessed to be immersed
By B. & D.'s embrace
Completely unrehearsed

You two are an iconic pair
An absolute authentic love
Blessed by the grace of God and his angels up above

25 years
Your love has been bound
To eternity
Your souls will be found

"Proverbs 27: Emotional Ascension"

"Open rebuke is better than secret love"
Have you experienced either sentiment above?

Outright arguing is much more freeing than harboring any intense feeling
Allowing the exchange to occur
Allowing the energy to transfer

Care motivates anger
Which means love is the anchor
Lifting us up to never be left as a cliffhanger

"Melted"

Do you focus on what you have or on what you've lost?

Are you encased in ice, waiting for the warmth of love to defrost?

What if you said, I don't need anyone else and the capacity to forgive is
within myself?

Don't you think all of that love should be shared and felt?

"Shared Particles"

My hope
Is for you to feel
My love

My hope
Is for you to internalize
My love

My hope
Is for you to act using
My love

My hope
Is for your love to become
My love